WOMEN EXPLORERS IN POLAR REGIONS

LOUISE ARNER BOYD, AGNES DEANS CAMERON, KATE MARSDEN, IDA PFEIFFER, HELEN THAYER

by Margo McLoone

Reading Consultant
Dr. Patricia Gilmartin, Ph.D.
Professor of Geography
University of South Carolina

CAPSTONE PRESS

MANKATO, MINNESOTA

C A P S T O N E   P R E S S
818 North Willow Street • Mankato, Minnesota 56001

Copyright © 1997 Capstone Press. All rights reserved. No part of this book may be reproduced without written permission from the publisher.

Printed in the United States of America.

Library of Congress Cataloging-in-Publication Data
McLoone, Margo.
    Women explorers in polar regions: Louise Arner Boyd, Kate Marsden, Ida Pfeiffer, Helen Thayer, Agnes Deans Cameron/by Margo McLoone.
    p. cm.--(Capstone short biographies)
    Includes bibliographical references and index.
    Summary: Briefly describes the lives and travels of five women who explored the polar regions.
    ISBN 1-56065-508-9
    1. Women explorers--Biography--Juvenile literature. 2. Arctic Regions--Discovery and exploration--Juvenile literature. [1. Explorers. 2. Women--Biography. 3. Arctic Regions--Discovery and exploration.] I. Title. II. Series.
G634.M38   1997
910'.82'0911--dc21
[B]
                                     96-45689
                                         CIP
                                         AC

Photo credits
Agnes Deans Cameron, 14, 18, 20
FPG, 33; Rosendo, 4; Green, 6
Helen Thayer, 36, 40
International Stock/Cliff Hollenbeck, cover, 30
Library of Congress, 28
Marin County Historical Society, 9, 12
Royal Geographic Society, London, 22 (D1839), 27 (B10533)

TABLE OF CONTENTS

CHAPTER 1

WHAT IS AN EXPLORER?

Explorers are people who want to learn about new and faraway places. They gather information about remote places and people. They usually write about their experiences, so others can learn.

Exploring versus Traveling

Explorers go places very few people have ever been. These lands are wild and sometimes dangerous. Usually there are no hotels or restaurants. Sometimes there are no roads. Then explorers must find or build their own paths.

Explorers must find or make their own paths.

Explorers in arctic areas are sometimes attacked by polar bears.

Traveling is different than exploring. Travelers usually go to places where there are other people. They stay in hotels and eat in restaurants. Travelers go places for pleasure.

Dangers Explorers Face

Explorers face many problems. The places they go are not on any maps. They use a compass. A compass tells them what direction they are going. But even with a compass, they can become lost.

Sometimes explorers climb high, icy mountains. Other explorers paddle down dangerous rivers. Often, they are attacked by wild animals. They cannot always find a hospital if they are hurt or sick.

Weather is also a danger. Blizzards, floods, or earthquakes can hurt explorers. It takes a long time for people to find and rescue a lost or injured explorer.

Women Explorers in the Polar Regions

When people think about explorers, they usually think of men. But many women have explored unknown lands. They have made important discoveries.

This book tells about the lives and experiences of five women explorers. They left their homes for adventure. These women explored the wilderness of the polar regions.

Their experiences have helped people learn about the animals, land, and cultures of the polar regions.

CHAPTER 2

LOUISE ARNER BOYD
1887—1972

Louise Arner Boyd was born on September 16, 1887, in San Rafael, California. Her family made a lot of money during the California gold rush.

Boyd had a comfortable childhood. She had her own maid. She rode horses and shot rifles on her family's ranch. As a teenager, she went on a tour of Europe and Africa.

But her childhood was not all happiness. Boyd was the only person in her family with

Louise Arner Boyd went on two arctic hunting trips. She shot 11 polar bears.

good health. Both of her younger brothers died of illnesses at early ages.

Boyd's mother died in 1919. Her father died in 1920. At the age of 33, she inherited a large fortune. She decided to travel.

She sailed on a tourist boat from Norway to the island of Spitsbergen. Spitsbergen is in the Arctic Ocean. It is near the North Pole.

Boyd was captivated by the frozen wilderness. She decided to explore the Arctic.

Looking for Amundsen

Boyd sailed to Franz Joseph Land for a hunting trip in 1925. The arctic islands that make up Franz Joseph Land are north of Russia. She shot three seals and 11 polar bears.

Boyd took a second hunting trip to the Arctic in 1927. But she never had a chance to hunt. Someone needed her help. A Norwegian explorer named Roald Amundsen was lost in the polar ice.

For four months, Boyd used her ship and crew to look for him. They traveled 10,000 miles (16,000 kilometers) along the arctic ice

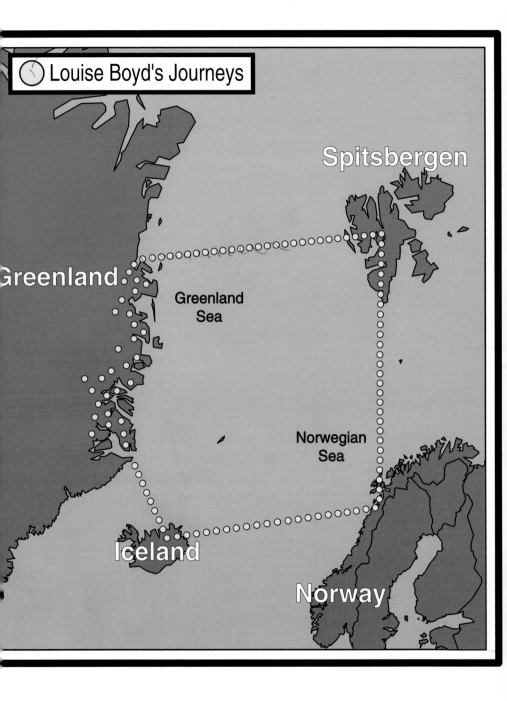

Louise Boyd's Journeys

Spitsbergen

Greenland

Greenland
Sea

Norwegian
Sea

Iceland

Norway

The U.S. Army used Boyd's maps in World War II.

pack. She took pictures and donated them to the American Geographic Society.

Finally, the search was called off. Amundsen was never found. Still, the King of Norway wanted to thank Boyd for searching. He gave her an award for her help.

Exploring for Science

Boyd returned to the Arctic and studied animals and plant life. She measured water depth. With special cameras, she photographed mountaintops and the sea floor. These photographs were made into valuable maps.

Boyd planned and paid for seven trips to the Arctic. She discovered an unknown glacier in Greenland. It was named Miss Boyd Land to honor her.

The United States Army used her maps of the Arctic during World War II (1939-1945). After the war, the U.S. Army honored Boyd for her contribution.

First Woman Arctic Explorer

Boyd was the first woman Arctic explorer. She proved that women could explore polar regions. She was a member of the United States' Society of Woman Geographers and Great Britain's Royal Geographic Society.

In 1972, Boyd died in a nursing home in California. Friends honored her last wishes to scatter her ashes over the Arctic.

CHAPTER 3

AGNES DEANS CAMERON
1863—1912

Agnes Deans Cameron was born in Victoria, British Columbia, Canada, in 1863. Cameron enjoyed learning. She became the first female high-school teacher in British Columbia. In 1894, she became the principal of South Park School.

In 1906, Cameron moved to Chicago to work for a newspaper. After two years, she decided to quit and become a travel writer.

Agnes Deans Cameron learned to hunt when she explored the Canadian wilderness.

Journey to the Arctic

Cameron left Chicago in May 1908. She planned to journey through Canada to the Arctic Ocean. She traveled with her niece, Jessie Cameron Brown. They became two of the first women to explore the Canadian wilderness.

Cameron decided to take photographs and write about her trip. She wanted to bring attention to the wilderness as a new frontier for immigrants. Immigrants are people who leave one country to live in another.

In six months, Cameron and Brown covered 10,000 miles (16,000 kilometers). They traveled by stagecoach, horseback, steamship, and scow. A scow is a wide, flat-bottomed boat with square ends.

Cameron followed the Mackenzie River during the short summer season. That way, she avoided winter ice. But she still had to survive mosquito season.

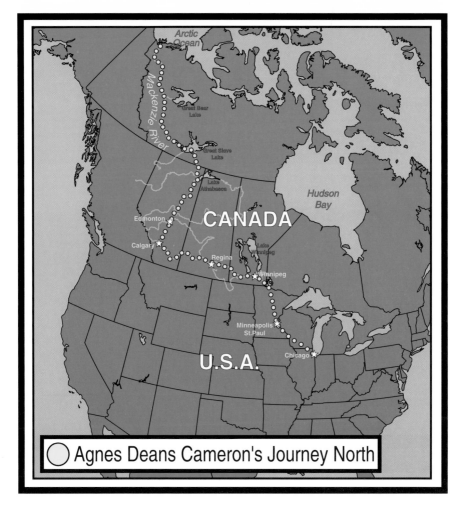

Agnes Deans Cameron's Journey North

Mosquito Season

Mosquitoes swarm during summers in the
Arctic. Sometimes they drive animals crazy.
Moose and deer often jump over cliffs or dive
into rivers to escape from the insects.

Cameron hunted and ate wild moose on her journey.

Cameron's native guides burned fires to keep mosquitoes away. But it did not work.

At night, Cameron tried to sleep by staying fully clothed. Despite the warm weather, she wrapped herself in a sleeping bag. She stayed under a net. Still, she was bitten many times.

Cameron knew that people in the North did not complain about harsh conditions or disasters. Cameron also did not complain about mosquitoes or other hardships.

Her exploration was full of danger. She traveled 90 miles (144 kilometers) down the river. Scows had to go over rapids and waterfalls. Sometimes they split in half. She saw one person drown.

For food, she ate moose nose and caribou tongue. Caribou is a type of deer. She also ate beaver tail and boiled beluga skin. Beluga is a type of whale.

Promoting the Arctic

Cameron wrote a book about her Arctic explorations. It was called *The New North*. After it was published, she toured Canada, Great Britain, and the United States. From 1909 to 1912, she told people about her adventures.

Cameron's talks detailed life in the Arctic. She described birds, animals, and insects that lived in the Arctic. She described burning coal

Cameron took notes while on her journey. Then she used the notes to give talks about life in the Arctic.

beds and tar pits that lined the shores of the Mackenzie River.

The Arctic is known as the land of the midnight sun. During certain times of the year, the sun shines at night. For Cameron, bedtime was at 4 A.M. and breakfast was at 4 P.M.

Cameron also described the food, religions, and social customs of the Inuit (IN-oo-wit) people. The Inuit are are Eskimo people from Canada and Greenland. She admired the Inuits' attitude toward hardship and life.

After the Arctic

Cameron traded with the Inuit and other native people for artifacts. Artifacts are things made by humans. They are usually used for practical tasks. She collected these artifacts and gave them to Canadian museums.

Cameron also wrote, traveled, and spoke about northwestern Canada. She encouraged people to settle in Canada's frontier.

In 1912, Cameron went to a hospital in British Columbia, Canada, to have her appendix removed. The operation was not a success. She died of complications from the surgery. Her photographs and collections are on display in Canada's national museums.

CHAPTER 4

KATE MARSDEN
1859—1931

Kate Marsden was born near London, England, on May 13, 1859. She was the youngest of eight children. Unlike her friends, Kate preferred climbing trees to sewing. Even when she was young, she wanted to go on adventures.

Her need for excitement led her to become a nurse. She attended a nursing school that sent its graduates to foreign countries. In 1877, Kate was sent to Bulgaria to care for soldiers at war. She went into battlefields to find wounded soldiers.

One day, Kate found a man hiding in an abandoned barn. His skin was lumpy and

Kate Marsden used her nursing skills to help lepers.

discolored. His nose and fingers had rotted and fallen off. He was blind.

The man suffered from leprosy (LEP-ruh-see). Leprosy is a disease that attacks the skin, nerves, and muscles. Body parts affected by leprosy often become paralyzed. People who have leprosy are usually called lepers.

The man had been sent away to suffer and die alone. At that time, people feared leprosy. They were afraid they might also become sick. So lepers were exiled. Exiled means that the person is sent away from his or her home or country and told not to return.

Marsden decided to help the man. She wanted to help other lepers, too.

On Sledge and Horseback

Marsden heard about a rare herb used to cure leprosy. It only grew in areas of Siberia, Russia. She knew that the herb was located by a leper colony near Viluisk (Vil-OOSK), Russia. She decided to journey to Viluisk. She wanted to find the herb and help the lepers.

In 1891, Marsden began a difficult journey across Russia. She traveled more than 11,000 miles (17,000 kilometers) to reach the northeast corner of Siberia.

A train took Marsden from Moscow to St. Petersburg. From there, she crossed Russia on a sledge. A sledge is a strong, heavy sled. Then she rode in a horse-drawn basket down the Siberian Post Road. She sailed the Lena River on a boat. Finally, she rode a horse for the remaining 2,000 miles (3,200 kilometers).

Dangerous Journey

Marsden had not imagined how difficult the trip would be. She carried a pistol. She had to deal with dishonest drivers. There was a constant threat of bear attacks. She suffered exhaustion and pain from the jarring trip.

Many times her sledge almost crashed through the ice of frozen rivers. She saw wild dogs fighting over dead horses. Wolves lined the sides of the road. She met chain gangs of prisoners trudging through snow and ice. She slept in filthy post stations.

Tea and Comfort

Marsden visited many leper colonies in Siberia. She brought hot tea and tinned food. She also brought comfort to the lepers. But the herb did not cure leprosy as Marsden had hoped.

Marsden returned to England. There she wrote *On Sledge and Horseback to Outcast Lepers* in 1893. This book told the story of her journey. She became a member of Great Britain's Royal Geographic Society in 1916.

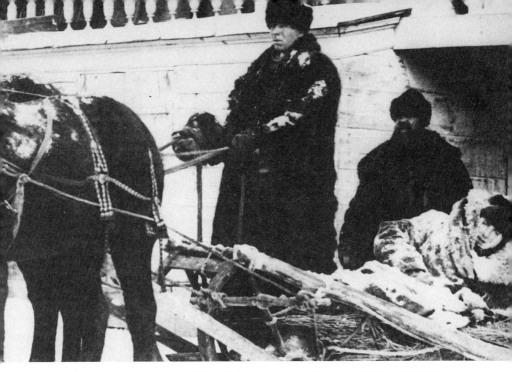

Marsden suffered pain and exhaustion from her rough journey on the sledge.

Marsden's book also helped raise money for lepers. She was not able to change the way society treated lepers. But she did help them. She opened a hospital for lepers in 1897. It was located in Viluisk.

Marsden's trip to Siberia was her last exploration. She was not able to recover from her exhausting journey. She spent the last 30 years of her life seriously ill. Marsden died in England in 1931.

CHAPTER 5

IDA PFEIFFER
1797—1858

Ida Reyer was born in Vienna, Austria, on October 14, 1797. She was the only girl among many brothers. Her father wanted her to be a boy, too. He educated, trained, and dressed her like a boy. She did not wear dresses until she became a teenager.

When Reyer was 22, she was pressured into marrying Dr. Pfeiffer, a rich widower. He was much older than Ida. They had two sons.

After 20 years of marriage, Pfeiffer separated from her husband. She had inherited some money from her mother. Her sons were

Ida Pfeiffer became the first woman travel writer.

Pfeiffer rode a camel across the Egyptian desert.

grown. So she decided to visit the places she
had always dreamed about.

To the Middle East

When Pfeiffer planned her first trip, she did not
think she would come back alive. She knew it
was dangerous for a woman to travel alone.
But that did not stop her. She wrote out her will
and prepared for her journey.

In 1842, she began her first trip. She told her family she was going to the Holy Land in present-day Israel. But she also wanted to visit other remote places.

Pfeiffer sailed down the Danube River into the Black Sea. She crossed the Black Sea and landed in Turkey. She went to Israel and then on to Egypt. In Egypt, she learned to ride a camel. She rode a camel across the desert and returned home.

She wrote *Journey of a Viennese Lady to the Holy Land* in 1843. This book earned her enough money for another trip.

Six Months in the Polar Regions

Pfeiffer explored Iceland for six months in 1845. She traveled in pony carts to Iceland's geysers (GYE-zurs) and hot springs. Geysers are holes in the ground. Bursts of hot water and steam shoot up from the holes.

Pfeiffer did not have much money. She had to live like a native Icelander. She stayed in Icelandic homes. She ate porridge and fish. She suffered from fleas in her bed.

Pfeiffer collected rocks and plants. She went home and sold her collection to museums. She also wrote *Journey to Iceland*, and *Travels in Sweden and Norway*. Her book and collections earned her more money. With it, she was able to pay for a trip around the world.

Trip Around the World

Pfeiffer sailed to South America in 1846. In two years, she traveled 35,000 miles (56,000 kilometers) by sea. She also journeyed 2,800 miles (4,480 kilometers) by land. She explored remote areas of South America, China, India, Iraq, Iran, and Russia.

In Brazil, South America, she hiked into the rain forest. She ate roast monkey with a tribe of Puri (PUR-ee) Indians. She was attacked by a thief. After that, she hid a gun in her clothes.

World Explorer

Unlike other European travelers of her time, Pfeiffer did not carry any luggage. All she brought was a leather bottle for water, salt, bread, rice, and a small pan to cook in. On her explorations, local people gave her food and shelter.

Pfeiffer's first trip around the world took her 19 months. The book about her journey was translated into English. It made her famous.

Ida Pfeiffer hunted tigers in India.

Pfeiffer went on tiger hunts in India. She crossed Iran on a camel. In Russia, she was mistaken for a spy and spent a night in jail.

Pfeiffer's book, *A Lady's Voyage Round the World* made her famous. People offered her free tickets to many remote places.

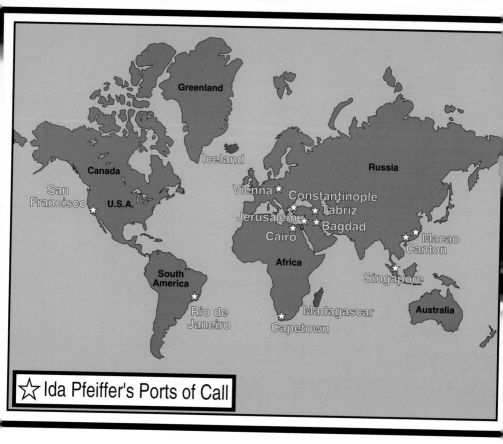

Second Trip Around the World

Pfeiffer sailed to the southern tip of Africa in 1851. From there, she began her second trip around the world.

She went to Borneo in the East Indies. She walked through a jungle to visit the Dyak (DYE-ak) tribe. The Dyak were feared headhunters. A headhunter is a person who cuts off an enemy's head. Then they preserve, shrink, and keep it to scare off evil spirits.

On the Indonesian island of Sumatra, Pfeiffer stayed with a cannibal tribe known as the Batak (BAY-tak). Cannibals are people who eat human flesh. After a while, the Batak threatened to eat her. Pfeiffer escaped from them. She was the first person who lived to write about the Batak.

Final Voyage
Pfeiffer went to Madagascar (Ma-dah-GA-skur) in 1857. This is an island off the coast of Africa. Madagascar's Queen Ranavalona (Ra-nah-vah-LOH-nah) put her in jail. The Queen forced Pfeiffer to play the piano for her.

Finally, Queen Ranavalona ordered Pfeiffer to leave Madagascar. But Pfeiffer was already sick with a tropical disease called Madagascar fever. She died in Vienna in 1858.

Pfeiffer overcame poverty to become a world traveler. She was the first professional woman travel writer. She wrote five popular travel books.

CHAPTER 6

HELEN THAYER
1938—

Helen Thayer was born in Whangarei (Wang-REE), New Zealand, in 1938. When she was nine years old, her parents helped her climb Mount Egmont. From then on, Thayer loved the challenge of mountain climbing.

Thayer climbed to the tops of the highest mountains around the world. But she wanted to keep exploring. So she decided to ski alone to one of the earth's poles. Besides being a mountain climber, Thayer was also a world-class athlete. But it still took her two years to prepare for her Arctic journey.

Helen Thayer decided to ski alone to one of the earth's poles.

Preparing for the Arctic

Thayer tested her equipment in cold, icy conditions. She learned about the movement of the magnetic North Pole.

The magnetic North Pole is the place to where all compass needles point. This pole can move many miles or kilometers in a few years. It is different from the geographic North Pole. The geographic North Pole is where the earth's lines of longitude meet.

Thayer trained with Inuit hunters. They taught her the ways of polar bears. The Inuit use dogs to protect them from polar bear attacks. They gave Thayer a black husky dog. She named him Charlie.

Most polar expeditions use snowmobiles or dog teams. They often have food and supplies brought to them by planes. But Thayer traveled on skis and pulled her supplies on a sled.

To the Magnetic North Pole

Thayer set out for the magnetic North Pole on March 30, 1988. She traveled on skis and pulled her supplies on a sled.

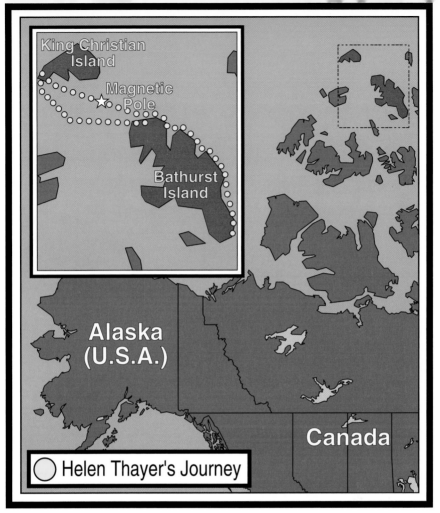

King Christian Island

Magnetic Pole

Bathurst Island

Alaska (U.S.A.)

Canada

◯ Helen Thayer's Journey

    She brought a tent, sleeping bag, stove,
radio to communicate with base camp, rifle,
flare gun, compass, map, camera, and food.
She ate rice, oatmeal, granola, peanut butter
cups, walnuts, milk, and chocolate powder. She
also took 85 pounds (38 kilograms) of dry dog
food for Charlie.

Helen Thayer's dog, Charlie, helped her survive three polar bear attacks.

Dangers of the Trip

It took Thayer 27 days to travel 364 miles (582 kilometers). She crossed frozen seas to reach the magnetic North Pole. During her journey, she almost fell into the freezing water. Frostbite blackened her fingers. Flying ice cut and bloodied her eyes. Wind swept away some of her food.

The greatest danger she faced was polar bears. Only her dog Charlie kept them away.

After surviving three polar bear attacks, Thayer cried tears of relief. Her eyelids instantly froze shut. It took an hour of defrosting before she could open her eyes.

Dream Come True

On April 21, 1988, Thayer became the first woman to reach the magnetic North Pole alone. She wrote *Polar Dream* about her journey.

Thayer returned to the magnetic North Pole with her husband Bill in 1992. They became the first and oldest married couple to reach it on foot.

After the Magnetic North Pole

In 1994, the Thayers explored 1,200 miles (1,920 kilometers) of remote Amazon jungle. Also in 1994, the Thayers walked 600 miles (960 kilometers) across the Canadian Yukon to study wolves.

Helen Thayer travels to schools to talk about her journeys. She has inspired many students to achieve their goals.

CHRONOLOGY

Ida Pfeiffer	Kate Marsden	Agnes Deans Cameron
1797	**1859**	**1863**
Born in Vienna, Austria	Born near London, England	Born in British Columbia, Canada
1842	**1877**	**1894**
Explores the Holy Land	Cares for wounded soldiers in Bulgaria	Becomes principal of South Park School
1845	**1891**	**1906**
Spends six months in Iceland	Journeys to Siberia, Russia, on a sledge	Moves to Chicago to write for a newspaper
1846	**1897**	**1908**
Begins first journey around the world	Opens a hospital for lepers in Viluisk, Russia	Leaves Chicago to journey to the Arctic
1851	**1916**	**1909—1912**
Begins second journey around the world	Becomes a member of Royal Geographic Society	Travels England, U.S.A., and Canada to talk about her adventures
1858	**1931**	**1912**
Dies in Vienna	Dies in England	Dies in British Columbia, Canada

Louise Arner Boyd

1887

Born in San Rafael, California, U.S.A.

1920

Inherits the family fortune; goes on first trip to the Arctic

1925

Sails to Franz Joseph Land for a hunting trip

1927

Helps search for Roald Amundsen

1939—1945

U.S. Army uses Boyd's maps during World War II

1972

Dies in San Francisco, California

Helen Thayer

1938

Born in Whangarei, New Zealand

1947

Climbs Mount Egmont

1988

Journeys to the magnetic North Pole

1992

Returns to magnetic North Pole with husband

1994

The Thayers explore remote Amazon jungles; they walk across the Yukon to study wolves

WORDS TO KNOW

artifact (ART-uh-fakt)—something made by humans, usually for a practical task

cannibal (KAN-uh-buhl)—a person who eats the flesh of other human beings

compass (KUHM-puhss)—an instrument used to determine geographic direction; it has a magnetic needle that points north.

headhunter (hed-HUHN-tur)—a person who cuts off an enemy's head, then preserves, shrinks, and keeps it to ward off evil spirits

Inuit (IN-oo-wit)—a member of the Eskimo peoples of North America

leprosy (LEP-ruh-see)—a disease that attacks the skin, nerves, and muscles

magnetic North Pole (MAG-net-ic NORTH POHL)—the place to where all compass needles point

TO LEARN MORE

Kalman, Bobbie. *The Arctic World Series*. New York: Crabtree Publishing, 1988.

Lepthien, Emile. *Greenland*. Chicago: Children's Press, 1989.

Matthews, Rupert. *Explorer*. London: Dorling Kindersley, 1991.

Rappaport, Doreen. *Living Dangerously: American Woman Who Risked Their Lives for Adventure*. New York: HarperCollins, 1991.

Stefoff, Rebecca. *Women of the World*. New York: Oxford University Press, 1992.

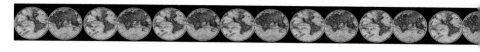

USEFUL
ADDRESSES

Information Center on Children's Cultures
332 East 38th Street
New York, NY 10016

National Geographic Society
1145 17th Street NW
Washington, DC 20036-4688

Royal Canadian Geographic Association
39 McArthur Avenue
Vanier, Ontario K1L 8L7
Canada

Society of Woman Geographers
415 East Capitol Street SE
Washington, DC 20003

INTERNET SITES

Arctic to Amazon Project
http://www.mukilteo.wednet.edu/MSD/HSPages/
ACES/ArcticToAmazon.html

Earthwatch
http://www.earthwatch.org

GlobaLearn
http://www.globalearn.org

Mountain Travel Sobek: Adventure Company
http://www.mtsobek.com

National Geographic Society
http://www.nationalgeographic.com/main.wd

INDEX